INTRO TO PHYSICS Need to Know

SilverTip

Matter

by Jane Parks Gardner

Consultant: Kathy Renfrew
Science Educator and Science Learner

BEARPORT
PUBLISHING

Minneapolis, Minnesota

Credits

Cover and title page, © Pixel-Shot/Shutterstock and © Stone36/Shutterstock; 5T, © Sandra Burm/Shutterstock; 5C, © 104000/Shutterstock; 5B, © Rattana Rattanawan/Shutterstock; 7T, © naluwan/Shutterstock; 7B, © kongkanglp/Shutterstock; 9, © Bacsica/Shutterstock; 10, © Santi S/Shutterstock; 11, © tomch/iStock; 13T, © Alter-ego/Shutterstock; 13B, © Vadim Gavrilov/Shutterstock; 15, © Firma V/Shutterstock; 17T, © Jiri Hera/Shutterstock; 17B, © Gus Andi/Shutterstock; 19T, © VallarieE/iStock; 19B, © Marco Zamperini/Shutterstock; 21, © S.Borisov/Shutterstock; 23, © Joshua Resnick/Shutterstock; 25, © barsik/iStock; 27T, © Cube And Live/Shutterstock; 27C, © apiguide/Shutterstock; 27B, © leeborn/Shutterstock; and 28, © Arisa_J/Shutterstock.

Bearport Publishing Company Product Development Team

President: Jen Jenson; Director of Product Development: Spencer Brinker; Senior Editor: Allison Juda; Editor: Charly Haley; Associate Editor: Naomi Reich; Senior Designer: Colin O'Dea; Associate Designer: Elena Klinkner; Product Development Assistant: Anita Stasson

Library of Congress Cataloging-in-Publication Data is available at www.loc.gov or upon request from the publisher.

ISBN: 979-8-88509-224-1 (hardcover)
ISBN: 979-8-88509-231-9 (paperback)
ISBN: 979-8-88509-238-8 (ebook)

Copyright © 2023 Bearport Publishing Company. All rights reserved. No part of this publication may be reproduced in whole or in part, stored in any retrieval system, or transmitted in any form or by any means, electronic, mechanical, photocopying, recording, or otherwise, without written permission from the publisher.

For more information, write to Bearport Publishing, 5357 Penn Avenue South, Minneapolis, MN 55419. Printed in the United States of America.

Contents

Matter, Matter Everywhere 4

The Smallest Parts 8

Do Me a Solid 10

Warming Up 12

Floating in the Sky 14

Hey, That's Different 16

Well, That's New 20

Something Synthetic 24

It's Everywhere 26

States of Matter 28

SilverTips for Success 29

Glossary 30

Read More 31

Learn More Online 31

Index 32

About the Author 32

Matter, Matter Everywhere

Look around. What do you see? Is there a flowering bush or a baseball flying through the sky? Maybe you see a tiny bird and its nest.

Everything you see has one thing in common. It's all **matter**.

Is it living or dead? It doesn't *matter* when it comes to matter. Matter makes up everything.

Big or small, matter is anything that takes up space and is made of *stuff*. We can measure all this stuff in **mass**. With a scale or a balance, we can see just how much matter is in something.

A pillow filled with feathers has less mass than a pillow filled with bricks. Both pillows may take up the same amount of space. But the stuff that makes up the pillow of bricks is heavier.

A heavy rock has more mass than a light balloon.

The Smallest Parts

All that *stuff* in things can be broken into very tiny parts. Matter is made of atoms. These building blocks of our universe come together to form **molecules**. Matter takes different forms, called **states**, based on its molecules. The main states are solid, liquid, and gas.

Your body contains three states of matter. Your bones and teeth are solids. Blood and saliva are liquids. You have oxygen and other gases in your body, too.

Models of Molecules

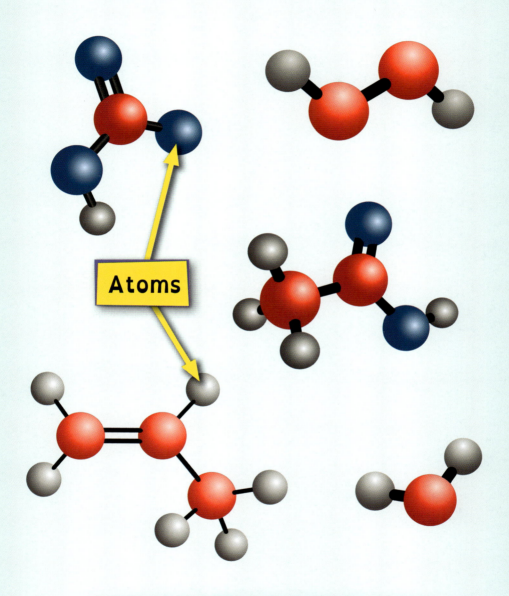

Atoms

Different kinds of atoms group together to form each molecule.

Do Me a Solid

Think about water. The same water molecules can act differently. Water can be in a solid state. We call it ice. The molecules in ice are close together and organized in lines. They move very slowly. You cannot even see the movement with your eyes.

Solids hold their shapes. But some can be bent, squashed, or broken. A glass vase can shatter into pieces if it's hit with enough force.

Warming Up

When ice melts, it changes from a solid to a liquid state. The molecules in liquids are farther apart. They move faster and more freely. Liquids do not have a definite shape. They can easily take the shape of their container.

If the temperature is high enough, many kinds of matter can be in a liquid state. Heat gold to 1,948 degrees Fahrenheit (1,064 degrees Celcius) and it will melt into a liquid!

Floating in the Sky

Water can be a gas, too. Boil water and it turns into steam. Steam is water in the gas state of matter. The molecules in a gas are far apart, and they move very fast. Gases will spread out to fill whatever space they have.

If a gas is heated to very, very high temperatures, a different type of matter forms. This is called plasma. Almost everything we can see in the night sky is plasma.

Hey, That's Different

Changing from one state to another is a **physical change**. The matter is the same. It's just in a different form.

A candy bar may melt from a solid to a liquid when left in the sun. But it is still made of chocolate.

Most physical changes are reversible. You can make a melted ice cube solid again by putting it in the freezer. Gases change to liquids in the clouds in our sky.

Physical changes can also affect the shape or texture of an object. Tearing paper into shreds is a physical change. Using sandpaper to smooth a piece of wood is, too. As long as nothing new is made, it is a physical change.

The molecules that make up the matter in physical changes stay the same. They may be separated into smaller groups, but how the atoms come together doesn't change.

Well, That's New

Matter changes into something new during a **chemical change**. The atoms within the molecules change and form different molecules.

Often, chemical changes will either take heat in or let it out. Some chemical changes make light or gases. Sometimes, there is a change in color or smell.

The Statue of Liberty in New York City changed colors. It started reddish brown and turned green. That is because the copper statue reacted with water and air in a chemical change.

Chemical changes can happen in different ways. But they share one thing in common. These changes are often **irreversible**. Once the change happens, it's nearly impossible to go back. That's because something new was made. The atoms in molecules have been rearranged.

Think of a chemical change as being like making cookies. You can't unbake a cookie. The ingredients can't be taken apart into piles of flour, sugar, or salt again.

Something Synthetic

Some chemical changes make **synthetic** materials. These start from **natural** resources, or things that are a part of Earth. Then, we change them into something that cannot be found in nature. For example, a chemical change turns fossil fuels into plastics.

Wool for warm winter socks is a natural material. A plastic sled used on a snowy day is synthetic. But the fossil fuels plastic comes from started as plants and animals that died long ago.

It's Everywhere!

Matter is all around us. Everything you see is an example of matter. It can take so many different forms. And matter can change from one form to another. But without matter, our world just wouldn't be the same . . . or exist at all!

Water is the only substance on Earth that can be found naturally as a solid, a liquid, and a gas. You find it frozen in icebergs, flowing over a waterfall, and in the air around the planet.

27

States of Matter

Solid

- Molecules in solids are packed tightly together.
- They hold their shape, and they do not move very much.

Liquid

- Liquids are a little more loosely packed.
- They can move or flow around to become the shape of their container.
- The parts of a liquid move around more than in solids.

Gas

- Gases move around the most.
- Their molecules are spread out.
- A gas can fill up an entire space.

SilverTips for SUCCESS

⭐ SilverTips for REVIEW

Review what you've learned. Use the text to help you.

Define key terms

atoms
chemical change
matter

molecules
physical change

Check for understanding

What is mass, and how does it relate to matter?

What are the three main states of matter?

Describe the differences between a physical change and a chemical change.

Think deeper

Think of at least one physical change you come across in your daily life and one chemical change you see regularly.

⭐ SilverTips on TEST-TAKING

- **Make a study plan.** Ask your teacher what the test is going to cover. Then, set aside time to study a little bit every day.

- **Read all the questions carefully.** Be sure you know what is being asked.

- **Skip any questions** you don't know how to answer right away. Mark them and come back later if you have time.

Glossary

atoms tiny things that make up every substance in the universe

chemical change a change in which the molecules in matter become something new

irreversible impossible to change back to how something was before

mass a measure of the amount or quantity of something

matter the material that makes up all objects

molecules small parts of matter that form when two or more atoms come together

natural made by nature

physical change a change in which matter changes form but is made of the same molecules

states ways or forms of being

synthetic made by humans rather than nature

Read More

Hulick, Kathryn. *Mixing and Measuring Matter (Science Masters).* North Mankato, MN: Rourke Educational Media, 2020.

Linde, Barbara Martina. *Atoms: It Matters (Spotlight On Physical Science).* New York: PowerKids Press, 2020.

Shea, Therese M. *Properties of Matter: It Matters (Spotlight on Physical Science).* New York: PowerKids Press, 2020.

Learn More Online

1. Go to **www.factsurfer.com** or scan the QR code below.
2. Enter "**Physics Matter**" into the search box.
3. Click on the cover of this book to see a list of websites.

Index

atom 8–9, 20, 22

chemical change 20, 22, 24

gas 8, 14, 16, 20, 26, 28

irreversible 22

liquid 8, 12, 16, 26, 28

mass 6–7

molecule 8–10, 12, 14, 18, 20, 22, 28

natural 24, 26

physical change 16, 18

plasma 14

solid 8, 10, 12, 16, 26, 28

states of matter 8, 10, 12, 14, 16, 28

synthetic 24

About the Author

Jane Parks Gardner has written more than 50 nonfiction books. She spends a lot of her time thinking about, reading about, writing about, and talking about science to anyone who will listen.